Ten Tiny Teddies

an alphabet book

This beautiful book will help to lay the early foundations for reading. Young children love words and often invent their own, savouring the sounds. They will enjoy having the rhymes and sentences read to them, as well as spotting objects in the pictures that start with the same sound.

Each page introduces a certain sound, so that children become aware of the different sounds that letters make. Early play with sounds, rhymes and letters is fun and a fundamental beginning to becoming a reader.

Children are never too young to enjoy words, letters and sounds. They make the pathway to reading both simple and joyful.

Pie Corbett

Pie Corbett
Poet and Consultant to the
National Literacy Strategy

This book also includes the common sounds ch, sh and th. There is a guide to pronouncing letter sounds on page 30, plus games to reinforce children's learning. You will find a list of words illustrated in the book on pages 31 and 32.

A

a

The acrobat annoys the angry alligator.

acrobat

axe

apple

arrow

alligator

anteater

antelope

ants

Why is the alligator angry?
What other animals can you see?

a b c d e f g h i j k l m n o p q r s t u v w x y z

Ten Tiny Teddies

an alphabet book

First published in the UK in 2000 by

Belitha Press Ltd
London House, Great Eastern Wharf,
Parkgate Road, London SW11 4NQ

ISBN 1 84138 202 7 (hardback)
ISBN 1 84138 210 8 (paperback)
ISBN 1 84138 205 1 (big book)

British Library in Publication Data for this book is available
from the British Library.

Series editors: Mary-Jane Wilkins, Stephanie Turnbull
Designers: Rachel Hamdi, Angie Allison
Illustrators: Louise Comfort, Charlotte Hard, Holly Mann
Educational consultants: Pie Corbett, Poet and Consultant
   to the National Literacy Strategy; Sarah Mullen, Literacy Consultant

Printed in Hong Kong / China

B

b

The boy and the baby are bouncing on the bed.

boy

bananas

bucket

boat

butterfly

bell

bull

bat

ball

balloon

What toys can you see?
What is the boy wearing?

a b c d e f g h i j k l m n o p q r s t u v w x y z

C

cat

castle

cup

camera

coat

The curious cat catches the canary.

[illustration of campers at a picnic by a camper van]

What are the campers going to eat?

What are the children doing?

C

cake

cap

carrot

cow

cage

a b c d e f g h i j k l m n o p q r s t u v w x y z

D

dinosaur

deer

dove

duck

donkey

Dogs and dinosaurs dancing at the disco.

d

door

dice

desk

dish

doll

Look for some other dancing animals.
What is on the desk?

abcd efghijklmnopqrstuvwxyz

E e

elf

The excited elves throw eggs at an elephant.

elephant

egg

envelope

elbow

elk

11
eleven

encyclopedia

How many elves are there?
What is each elf doing?

abcde f g h i j k l m n o p q r s t u v w x y z

F f

The fat farmer follows the feathers across the field.

farmer

fox

feather

fish

fire

fence

fork

forest

farm

feet

What does the farmer look like?
Who is he chasing?

abcde**f**ghijklmnopqrstuvwxyz

G

goat

girl

guitar

goldfish

The guilty goats guzzle in the garden.

g

gate

goggles

garage

goose

How did the goats get into the garden?
What is the boy doing?

abcdefghijklmnopqrstuvwxyz

H h

The hot, hungry horses hurry up the hill.

horse

hen

hay

hill

hive

house

helicopter

hammer

hat

hare

What are the horses going to eat?

Who is hiding in the hedge?

a b c d e f g h i j k l m n o p q r s t u v w x y z

I i

The **inky iguana** issues **important invitations.**

iguana

ill

ink

invitation

insects

indigo

What is on the iguana's desk?
How is the girl feeling?

abcdefgh i jklmnopqrstuvwxyz

J

jester

jar

jug

jeans

jacket

The jester juggles with jugs and jars.

j

jaguar

jeep

jet

jigsaw puzzle

jack-in-the-box

What are the children wearing?
What toys are they playing with?

a b c d e f g h i j k l m n o p q r s t u v w x y z

K k

Ouch! The kangaroo kicks the king.

king

kangaroo

key

kitten

koala

kite

kid

What has the king dropped?
What is the girl doing?

abcdefghij k lmnopqrstuvwxyz

The lazy lion licks the luscious lollipop.

l

lion

log

leaf

lamb

ladder

lantern

lizard

lemon

leopard

lollipop

What is the lady doing?
What is on the tree?

abcdefghijklmnopqrstuvwxyz

The magician meets a mermaid in a maze.

 M

m

monster

mermaid

mouse

mushroom

mug

monkey

mask

map

mirror

moon

Who is following the magician?
What is the mermaid holding?

a b c d e f g h i j k l m n o p q r s t u v w x y z

N n

Nine naughty newts saw a necklace in the nursery.

newt

nest

nut

necklace

1 2 3
numbers

nightdress

newspaper

notebook

nose

night

What is on the chest of drawers?
What is the baby wearing?

abcdefghijklmnopqrstuvwxyz

An octopus offers an orange to an otter.

ostrich

otter

orange

octagon

octopus

omelette

orang-utan

olive

Who else is in the café?
What is the ostrich about to eat?

abcdefghijklmnopqrstuvwxyz

P p

A pair of puppies pounce on the pizzas.

puppy

pineapple

parachute

piano

pear

parrot

puppet

peacock

pizza

panda

What is on the table?

What can you see outside?

abcdefghijklmno p qrstuvwxyz

Q q

The duck quacks at
the quarrelsome queen.

queen

queen

quiver

quartet

quail

quill pen

quadruplets

quilt

What is the queen holding?
What gifts are people carrying?

abcdefghijklmnopqrstuvwxyz

R r

The robber rats are rowing down the river.

rat

rattle

rope

roller skate

ring

rug

radio

rose

rocket

robot

What have the robbers stolen?
Who is on the river bank?

a b c d e f g h i j k l m n o p q r s t u v w x y z

S

S

Six silly sailors selling socks by the sea.

sock

sun

surfer

sandal

sandwich

sandcastle

suitcase

seal

sack

submarine

What are the sailors going to eat?
What can you see behind them?

T teddy

tent

table

t-shirt

toothbrush

Ten tired teddies are ready for their bed.

t

tomato

towel

tortoise

telescope

teapot

What are the teddies doing?
Who can you see under the table?

a b c d e f g h i j k l m n o p q r s t u v w x y z

U V

Under his umbrella, the vulture visited the vet.

umbrella

vulture

van

vase

volcano

vegetables

veil

violin

violet

village

What is on the vet's desk?
What can you see outside?

uv

abcdefghijklmnopqrst uv wxyz

W

witch

wolf

well

window

waterfall

The wild wolf watches the wicked witch washing.

What is in the witch's garden?
What is the weather like?

W

web

windmill

woods

wall

worm

abcdefghijklmnopqrstuvwxyz

xyz

yak

yacht

yo-yo

yam

yoghurt

**Can you find
a fox on a box,
a yam on a yak
and a zebra in the zoo?**

xyz

zebra

zigzag

zip

zither

abcdefghijklmnopqrstuvw

xyz

ch

chimpanzee

The cheerful cheetah chases the cheeky chimps.

ch

child

chest

chair

chimney

cherry

chocolate

chicken

chess

cheetah

What are the other chimps doing?
What have they brought to eat?

sh

The shaggy sheep show off their shirts and shorts.

sh

sheep

shepherd

shed

shirt

shoes

shell

shark

ship

shovel

shorts

What is on the shelf?
Where is the shy sheep?
What is in the sea?

th th

Three thin thieves throw a throne into a thorn bush.

thief

thread

thumb

throne

theatre

thimble

thorn

What is the queen carrying?
Why is one thief holding a glass?
What is on the shelf?

Notes for parents and teachers

Children need to learn the sound that represents each letter.
They can confuse the sound with the name of the letter when reading.
Letter names do not help children read and spell and can be learned later.
So the letter e should sound like e as in egg, rather than e as in eat.
The sounds should be either clipped as in b or run on as in sssss.
This list will help you to pronounce the sounds correctly.

a as in cat		p as in pit	
b as in ball		q as in queen	say as qu
c as in cat		r as in rat	rrrrr like an angry dog
d as in dog		s as in sit	ssssss like a snake
e as in pet		t as in tap	
f as in foot	fffff	u as in mug	
g as in gate		v as in van	vvvvvv
h as in hat	like a dog panting	w as in wet	
i as in pig		x as in fox	say as ks
j as in jam		y as in yet	
k as in king		z as in zoo	zzzzz like someone snoring
l as in lap	lllllll	sh as in shop	sssshhhhhh
m as in mix	mmmm	th as in thin	
n as in nut	nnnnnn	ch as in chip	
o as in log			

Here are two activities to help children hear the sounds at the start of words.

Think of another
Choose a sound. How many objects can you think of that begin with the same sound?

Odd one out
Say three words that begin with the same sound and one that doesn't. Which one is the odd one out?

Word list

Here are all the words illustrated in this book.

Aa
accident
acrobat
across
alligator
ambulance
angry
animal
annoy
ant
anteater
antelope
ants' nest
apple
arrow
asleep
axe

Bb
baby
badge
ball
balloon
banana
bandage
bare (feet)
basket
bat
beach ball
bear
bed
bedroom
bee
beetle
bell
belt
big
bird
blanket
blue
boat
book
bookshelf
boots
bottle
bottom

bounce
bowl
boy
bucket
bull
bunch
bus
buttercup
butterfly
button

Cc
cabbage
cage
cake
calf
camera
camper
camping
camping
   stove
can
canary
candle
cap
caravan
card
cardigan
carrot
castle
cat
catch
cauliflower
coat
coffee
cola
comic
cooking
corn
countryside
cow
cucumber
cup
curious
curtain
cushion

Dd
dachshund
dalmation
dance
dawn
deer
desk
dice
dinosaur
diplodocus
dirty
disco
dish
dog
doll
donkey
door
doughnut
dove
duck

Ee
egg
elbow
elephant
eleven
elf
elk
embrace
empty
encyclopedia
envelope
excited

Ff
farm
farmer
farmhouse
fat
feather
fence
fern
field
fir tree
fire
fish

fist
follow
foot
forest
fork
fox
frog
furious
furrow
furry

Gg
gap
garage
garden
gardener
gate
girl
glove
goat
goggles
golden
goldfish
goose
guilty
guitar
gull
gutter
guzzle

Hh
hair
hammer
hand
handkerchief
hare
hat
hay
head
heart
hedge
helicopter
hen
hide
high
hill

hit
hive
hole
hoof
horse
hose
hot
house
hungry
hurry
hut
hutch

Ii
iguana
ill
important
indigo
ink
inky
insect
instrument
invitation
issue
itchy

Jj
jacket
jack-in-
   the-box
jaguar
jam
jar
jeans
jeep
jester
jet
jigsaw puzzle
jug
juggle
juice
jump

Kk
kangaroo
kettle

key
kick
kid
king
kiosk
kite
kitten
koala

Ll
ladder
lady
lake
lamb
lantern
large
lawn
lazy
leaf
lean
lemon
leopard
letter
lick
lid
lie
lift
lion
lizard
lobster
log
lollipop
lunch
luscious

Mm
magician
map
march
mask
match
mattress
maze
meet
melon
mermaid

middle
mirror
money
monkey
monster
moon
moonlight
mountain
mouse
moustache
muddy
mug
mushroom

Nn
nail
naughty
near
necklace
nest
net
newspaper
newt
night
nightdress
nine
nose
notebook
number
nurse
nursery
nut
nutcracker

Oo
octagon
octopus
offer
olive
omelette
orange
orang-utan
ostrich
otter

Pp
pair
palm tree
pancake

panda
parachute
parachutist
parcel
park
parrot
party
pasta
pea
peach
peacock
peanut
pear
pearl
piano
picture
pie
pig
pile
pillar
pineapple
pink
pizza
plant
plate
pond
potato
pounce
present
Punch and
  Judy
puppet
puppy
purple

Qq
quack
quadruplet
quail
quarrelsome
quartet
queen
quill pen
quilt
quiver

Rr
rabbit
radio
rake
rat
rattle
red
reed
ring
river
robber
robot
rock
rocket
rod
roller skate
rope
rose
row
rowing boat
rug

Ss
sack
sail
sailing boat
sailor
salad
sale
salt
sand
sandal
sandcastle
sandwich
satchel
sausage
sea
seal
seaside
seat
sell
silly
sit
six
sock
submarine
suitcase
sun
sunglasses

sunhat
surfboard
surfer

Tt
table
talk
tantrum
teacher
teapot
tear
teddy
teeth
telescope
ten
tent
tired
tomato
toothbrush
toothpaste
tortoise
towel
t-shirt

Uu
umbrella
under

Vv
valentine
vampire
van
vase
vegetable
veil
vet
video
videotape
village
vine
violet
violin
viper
visit
vixen
volcano
vulture

Ww
wall
wand
wash
washing
washing line
watch
waterfall
web
weed
well
wet
wicked
wild
windmill
window
windy
witch
wolf
wood
worm

Xx
box
fox

Yy
yacht
yak
yam
yawn
yell
yellow
yoghurt
yo-yo

Zz
zebra
zigzag
zip
zither
zoo

Ch
chair
chase
checked
cheeky
cheerful
cheese

cheetah
cherry
chess
chest
chicken
child
chimney
chimpanzee
chocolate
chunk

Sh
shade
shadow
shaggy
shark
sharp
shears
shed
sheep
shelf
shell
shelter
shepherd
shiny
ship
shirt
shoe
shore
shorts
shout
shovel
show off
shut
shy

Th
theatre
thief
thimble
thin
thirsty
thorn
thread
three
throne
through
throw
thumb